ROTHERHAM PUBLIC LIBRARIES

This book must be returned by the date specified at the time of
issue as the Date Due for Return.
The loan may be extended (personally, by post or telephone) for
a further period, if the book is not required by another reader,
by quoting the above number   LM1 (C)

REVOLUTION!

1848: YEAR OF REVOLUTION

R. G. Grant

Wayland

R E V O L U T I O N !

1848: Year of Revolution
The American Revolution
The Easter Rising
The French Revolution
Revolution in Europe, 1989
The Russian Revolution

Cover picture: *The storming of Berico during the Battle of Vicenza in June 1848.*
Title page: *Workers clash with the National Guard in Vienna.*
Contents page: *Demonstrators in Berlin meet the brutal Prussian Army in March 1848.*

Series editor: Paul Mason
Designer: Stonecastle Graphics Ltd
Picture researcher: Gerrie Nicholls

First published in 1995 by Wayland (Publishers) Ltd,
61 Western Road, Hove, East Sussex BN3 1JD, England

British Library Cataloguing in Publication Data
Grant, RG
1848: Year of Revolution. - (Revolution!
Series)
I.Title II.Series
940.284

ISBN 0 7502 1476 7

Typeset by Stonecastle Graphics Ltd, Marden, Tonbridge, Kent, England
Printed and bound by G. Canale & C.S.p.A., Turin, Italy

Picture Acknowledgements
The publishers would like to thank the following for permission to use their pictures in this book (t = top, b = bottom, l = left, r = right): AKG London 1, 3, 4, 6–7, 9, 11, 12–13, 13, 14, 15, 22, 22–3b, 27, 28 (both), 30b; e t archive 16, 32, 33, 40–41; Bridgeman Art Library cover, 8–9, 21b, 25, 36, 37, 44; Mary Evans Picture Library 6b, 7b, 10, 17, 20–21, 24–5, 29, 38, 40; Explorer 18b (ES), 39 (Hilda), 43 (JL); Fotomas Index 31; Robert Harding Picture Library 23t; Hulton Deutsch Collection 30t, 34 (both), 35; L'Illustration/Sygma 18–19, 26; Ann Ronan Picture Library 5; Popperfoto 45. Maps were provided by Peter Bull.

CONTENTS

UPRISING

Revolution in Paris

On the dark winter evening of 23 February 1848, a long procession advanced slowly through the ill-lit streets of central Paris. These were the working people of the city – men in overalls, many with the grime of the workshop still on their hands, and poorly dressed women with their barefoot children. Some carried flaming torches to light their way, and a red flag flapped over the heads of the crowd.

They were marching to celebrate a victory. The unpopular French king, Louis Philippe, had given in to demands for reform. He had agreed to appoint a new government and to make France a little more democratic. These were changes that had been demanded by middle-class liberals – people who were comfortably off and very different from the poor who were demonstrating in the street. But the king had only conceded the reforms because the working people of Paris had rioted the previous day and threatened to become uncontrollable.

Parisian revolutionaries attack a government building on 24 February 1848. The February Revolution in France set off a chain reaction throughout Europe.

TIMELINE

1848
12 January
Revolt against Bourbon rule in Palermo, Sicily.
23 February
Demonstrators are fired on by troops in Paris.
24 February
King Louis Philippe of France abdicates.
26 February
The Second Republic is proclaimed in France.
5 March
German liberals call for an all-German assembly to meet in Frankfurt.
13 March
Prince Metternich is driven from power in Austria.
18 March
Milan rises up against the Austrians, who are driven out after five days' street fighting.
19 March
King Frederick William of Prussia capitulates to demonstrators and announces reforms.

EYEWITNESS: PARIS IN REVOLUTION

Alphonse de Lamartine, a famous romantic poet and a member of the Provisional Government that replaced Louis Philippe, witnessed the excited revolutionary crowd that invaded the Chamber of Deputies on 24 February 1848: *'They crowded the corridors, and rushed with their cries of mortal combat into the spectators' galleries. Their clothes torn, their shirts open, their arms bare, their fists clenched and resembling muscular clubs, their hair wildly dishevelled and singed with cartridges, their countenances maddened with the delirium of revolution, their eyes smitten with the spectacle, so novel to them, presented by this Chamber . . . all revealed them to be desperadoes, who were come to make the last assault on the last refuge of royalty.'*

An unruly mob pours through the streets of Paris, revolting against King Louis Philippe.

Alexis de Tocqueville, a liberal aristocrat and historian, described Paris the day after the revolution: *'I spent the whole afternoon wandering about Paris and was particularly struck by . . . how little hatred was shown in this first moment of victory by the humble people who had suddenly become the sole masters of power . . . The people alone bore arms, guarded public buildings, watched, commanded and punished; it was an extraordinary and terrible thing to see the whole of this huge city, full of so many riches . . . in the hands of those who owned nothing.'*

France had no effective police force, so soldiers were stationed all over Paris to keep order in this threatening situation. As the torchlit procession headed down the Boulevard des Capucines that winter evening, its path was blocked by solid ranks of the king's troops, who were protecting government buildings. Their commander, on horseback in front of the soldiers, ordered them to fix bayonets. Soon the people at the front of the march were only a few metres from the sharp bayonet points.

Suddenly, perhaps frightened by the torches and the flapping red banner, the commander's horse reared and plunged back into the ranks of the troops. A volley of shots rang out, echoing between the high buildings. No one had given the order to fire, but in an instant of confusion some of the soldiers had started to shoot, and others joined in. It was a massacre. Men, women and children fled in panic, desperately seeking somewhere to hide from the bullets. The cries and groans of the wounded and dying filled the night. Within minutes, the

HUNGER AND POVERTY

In 1848 Europe was a discontented and unstable continent. Its population had doubled in a hundred years and its great cities were swelled by a mass of immigrants from the country in search of work. There was not enough housing for all these people. Many lived in squalid, overcrowded slums with no sanitation and inadequate food. Disease was rife – outbreaks of cholera killed tens of thousands. In some poor areas the average age of death was 30.

The condition of the people in Europe had worsened through a terrible crisis in the 1840s. It started with agriculture. The harvests between 1845 and 1847 were poor. In particular, a blight destroyed most of the continent's potato crop. The potato blight brought hunger to many parts of Europe – in Ireland a famine killed half a million people. Food prices doubled in many cities. People who struggled to survive in normal times were pushed to the brink of starvation. Even those who could still afford to eat ended up with less money to spend on other goods. This depressed

the whole economy, because producers could not sell their goods. Firms went bankrupt and their workers were thrown out on the street.

By 1848 the worst of the economic crisis was over. But people did not know this. They were angry and frightened and blamed their governments for failing to guarantee food and work. There was a general feeling that a radical change was needed, although there were many different ideas of what that change should be.

Revolutionaries storm the Tuileries, King Louis Philippe's palace, in the heart of Paris. The king fled the country to escape the anger of his people.

boulevard was deserted except for the soldiers and those who had been shot. Fallen torches, dropped by fleeing marchers, lit the heaps of corpses and pools of blood on the cobblestones garishly. About 40 people were dead.

Once the panic was over, shocked demonstrators returned to gather up the corpses. They piled the bodies on to carts and wheeled them through the streets of Paris to show people what had been done. They deliberately exposed the terrible wounds to public view: blood dripped on to the cartwheels and left a trail behind them as they went.

Fired with indignation at the massacre, the people of Paris rose in revolt. Piling up everything movable they could find – barrels, paving stones, wooden beams, overturned carts – they built huge barricades to block the narrow, winding streets of the poor districts where they lived. If the king was going to regain control, his troops would have to attack the barricades. But the soldiers hesitated to make war on their fellow Frenchmen. The National Guard, an armed force of part-time volunteers – mostly made up of better-off citizens, who could afford the time and the equipment – was supposed to help restore order. Most of the National Guard had no time for King Louis Philippe, however. They stayed neutral or even sided with the people. On the afternoon of 24 February, lacking any effective support, the king abdicated and fled.

Right *King Louis Philippe abdicates the French throne on 24 February 1848. Ironically he himself had come to power 18 years earlier as the result of a popular uprising in Paris.*

Left *Slums in Bloomsbury, London. In 1848 all the fast-growing cities of Europe had disease-ridden slums like this, where poor people lived in overcrowded conditions. Whole families had to squeeze into one small room.*

Now Paris was in the hands of its citizens. An unruly mob of people invaded the royal palace of the Tuileries and threw Louis Philippe's throne into the courtyard. They also stormed into the Chamber of Deputies, France's parliament, brandishing pikes and sabres. A new Provisional Government was being formed by politicians and journalists who had opposed Louis Philippe. Some of them would have preferred to choose another king to rule in Louis Philippe's place, but the mob demanded a republic. They wanted no more kings.

Production boomed throughout Europe during the Industrial Revolution, but these workers toiled long hours, often in poor conditions.

THE NEW FACTORIES

In 1848 Europe was in the early stages of the Industrial Revolution. The new factories increased vastly the amount of goods that could be produced in a day. They would eventually make Europe far more prosperous. But in the short term they made many poor people's lives even harder. Industrial workers toiled for low wages under harsh discipline, fourteen hours a day, six days a week.

Outside Britain and Belgium, there were as yet only a small number of factories, but the new machines were changing everyone's lives. In particular the artisans – craft workers who owned the tools of their trade and worked in small workshops – could see the writing on the wall. They would not be able to compete with cheaper machine-produced industrial goods.

Although industrial workers suffered very bad pay and living conditions, they played only a small part in the 1848 revolutions. It was the artisans, along with the poorest people in the cities who had neither proper work nor proper food, who provided the shock troops for the revolutionary street fighting.

Right Frederick William IV, King of Prussia, was an absolute monarch, convinced of his divine right to rule his country. During the 1848 revolution he was forced to make humiliating concessions to his people.

The mob forced the middle-class politicians to include Alexandre Albert, an ordinary working man, in the new government. And they insisted that Louis Blanc, a socialist who was popular with many working people, should also join the government. For the moment, the politicians were too afraid of popular violence to resist. Paris was in the grip of revolution, and no one knew where it would lead.

The copycat revolutions

As news of the dramatic events in Paris spread across Europe, carried by mail coaches, messengers on horseback and the new electric telegraph, it brought a surge of hope to all those who longed for change. If the people of Paris could overthrow their government, why couldn't the people of Vienna, Milan or Berlin? Throughout Germany, the Austrian Empire and Italy, the governments of kings and aristocrats feared for their survival. A tidal wave of revolution threatened to sweep them away.

The German lands

Until 1870, Germany was a loose confederation of separate states, each ruled by its own prince or king. By far the most powerful German ruler was the king of Prussia, Frederick William IV. He was already under attack from liberals demanding reform when the news of the Paris revolution arrived. The situation in the Prussian capital, Berlin, became very tense over the following weeks, especially after 400 workers were sacked from a large engineering works hit by the economic crisis. On 18 March the king tried to head off discontent by announcing minor reforms. But that same day his troops clashed with demonstrators and barricades went up throughout Berlin.

The Prussian Army's response to the revolt was ruthless and brutal. It attacked with all the force at its disposal, raking the densely populated streets with cannon and rifle fire. The workers and students who manned the barricades defended themselves bravely against the advancing troops, mostly with makeshift weapons – pitchforks, rusty sabres, even planks of wood. Children posted on the rooftops rained stones down on the soldiers' heads. When a street was retaken by the army, they hauled everyone they could lay hands on away to prison. An eyewitness described how the prisoners were maltreated by the soldiers, 'dragged away under constant blows with the rifle butt and the flat of the sabre.'

Berliners defend their barricades against advancing Prussian soldiers in March 1848.

The army regained control of the centre of Berlin. But public opinion was against the king. He lacked the will to drown the uprising in blood, and on 19 March Frederick William suddenly called off the troops and gave in to demands for reform. In a gesture of humiliating surrender, the haughty king of Prussia appeared in public draped in the black, red and gold flag of Germany, the symbol of the German revolution.

The less important German princes were in no position to resist where the king of Prussia had failed. Middle-class liberals thought these old-fashioned princely courts made Germany backward and powerless. They wanted to unify Germany under a single parliamentary government. Inspired by events in Paris, on 5 March a meeting of liberals called for representatives from all the German states to assemble at Frankfurt. This assembly, which met on 30 March, agreed to hold national elections for a German parliament. This was a genuinely revolutionary move. If it succeeded, it would transform the map of Europe.

Collapse of the Habsburgs

The hard core of resistance to revolution in Europe should have been in the Austrian capital, Vienna. From there the Habsburg emperor, Ferdinand, and his chief minister,

METTERNICH'S EUROPE

At the Congress of Vienna in 1814-15, at the end of the Napoleonic wars, diplomats created a new European order. It was consciously designed to block the path to freedom and democracy. The architect of this new order was the Austrian statesman Prince Klemens von Metternich.

Metternich had witnessed some of the excesses of the French Revolution of 1789 and hated popular upheaval above all things. He tried to convince all the monarchs of Europe that they should support one another to keep things exactly as they were. However incompetent or unpopular a ruler might be, Metternich believed he should be supported on the grounds of 'legitimacy'. Metternich also hated nationalism. In his system there was no place for a united Italy or Germany. He once described Italy as merely 'a geographical expression'.

Metternich's system prevailed in Europe for over 30 years. But it could not allow for necessary change, and ultimately was sustained only by force, not by consent.

Above *Prince Klemens von Metternich, the Austrian chancellor, hoped to maintain order in Europe by keeping things just as they were.*

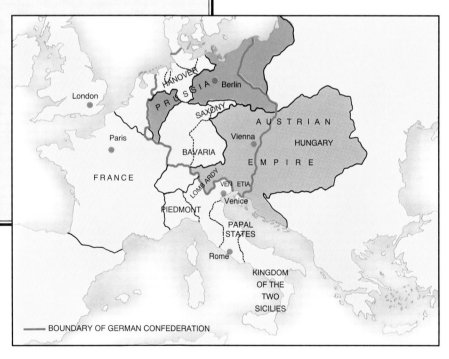

— BOUNDARY OF GERMAN CONFEDERATION

Prince Klemens von Metternich, used police spies, political prisons and censorship to control a huge empire, which included Hungary and much of northern Italy. But the empire was rotten at its heart. Emperor Ferdinand was mentally subnormal and incompetent, and the once mighty Metternich, now 74 years old, was the target of devious plots by his enemies at court.

The borders of Europe were set by the Congress of Vienna of 1814-15 through a series of deals between rulers.

LIBERALS AND WORKERS

In the spring of 1848 the middle classes – people like doctors, businessmen, lawyers, teachers, civil servants, students and journalists – were mostly on the side of the revolution. They supported 'liberalism', believing their countries needed elected parliaments to limit the power of the kings, and individual freedoms protected by the law. They felt that the conservative monarchies were holding back modernisation and economic progress.

The middle classes' desire for change led them into an alliance with the workers and the poor, who also wanted to overthrow the system. But in the end the interests of these two groups were completely different. The poor and hungry had nothing to lose from disorder, whereas the middle classes feared for their property and wanted order restored as soon as possible. And the workers wanted social change, to give themselves better food and housing and more control over their own lives. But this could only be at the expense of the middle-class factory owners and businessmen, who profited from cheap labour.

The middle-class liberals were happy to exploit popular uprisings to win concessions from the conservative rulers. But later they would support the use of force against the people to restore order.

On 3 March a bold Hungarian aristocrat, Lajos Kossuth, spoke in the Hungarian Diet (a kind of parliament) at Bratislava. He attacked Habsburg rule and called for the right of Hungarians to run their own government. At the same time, in Vienna, liberals demanded an end to the absolute rule of the emperor, real power for parliament and an end to censorship.

On 13 March workers and students threw up barricades in the streets of Vienna. Metternich's enemies in the royal court forced him to resign. Leaving Vienna for his own safety, Metternich fled to refuge in England. Two days later the emperor surrendered to the people. He promised major reforms and gave Hungary a large measure of independence. Meanwhile the Slavs in Prague had also asked for self-rule. The mighty Austrian Empire was threatening to fall apart.

Below *The National Guard, part-time soldiers, demonstrate against the Austrian emperor in Vienna in March 1848.*

Above *Milanese citizens defend their position against the oncoming Austrian Army. Almost the entire population of Milan fought a five-day battle against the might of the Austrian Army – and won.*

The struggle for Italy

When the Austrian army commanders in northern Italy learned of the uprising in Vienna, they knew their position was shaky. Marshal Radetzky in Milan and General Zichy in Venice were both controlling rebellious Italians who hated Austrian rule. General Zichy had the worst problem because many of his troops were Italian. They were unlikely to kill their fellow Italians. When Venice rose in revolt, Zichy soon surrendered. A Venetian patriot, Daniel Manin, proclaimed Venice a republic and the Austrian Army left the city.

Radetzky, however, was a tougher and more ruthless commander than Zichy. He was not prepared to leave Milan without a fight. The Milanese people rose up against the Austrians on 18 March, determined to drive the foreigners out of their city. For five heroic days, they fought against 13,000 well-armed troops in desperate close combat. The city was rocked by the roar of cannon fire and the rattle of rifles. Contorted bodies lay at street corners or stretched across the rubble of the barricades.

RULERS OF ITALY

In 1848 Italy was a hotchpotch of different states. Sicily and Naples were ruled by the cruel, inefficent Bourbon king, Ferdinand II. In the centre were several small dukedoms and the Papal States, an area ruled by the Pope from Rome. Lombardy and Venetia were directly controlled by the Austrians. And the northwest of Italy was ruled by the deeply conservative king of Piedmont and Sardinia, Charles Albert. All these states were oppressed by press censorship and police spies. There were no elected parliaments.

Revolutionary stirrings began as early as 1846. A new Pope, Pius IX, introduced some mild liberal reforms that excited hopes of change throughout the country. In January 1848 there was a revolt against the Bourbons in Sicily, and Ferdinand II was forced to grant a constitution. Rulers further north also began to rush through concessions to liberal demands. By the time the news of the February revolution in Paris arrived, the whole of Italy was already in ferment.

Left *In 1848 revolutions broke out right across Italy, from Palermo in the south, where the first uprising occurred in January, to Venice and Milan in the north. No ruler felt safe – not even Pope Pius IX, ruler of the Papal States.*

Below *Marshal Joseph Radetzky led the Austrian Army against the people of Milan in March 1848. He was driven out of the city by the uprising but later triumphed over the revolutionaries.*

THE DOWNFALL OF LOLA MONTEZ

In February 1848 King Ludwig, the ruler of Bavaria in southern Germany, had got into serious difficulties through his infatuation with his mistress, a beautiful Irish-American adventuress known as Lola Montez (her real name was Maria Gilbert). Ludwig enraged many of his subjects by making her 'Countess of Landsberg' and letting her influence state policy. Students stoned Lola's house in the Bavarian capital, Munich, and the king responded by threatening to close down the university.

The news of the Paris revolution arrived in the middle of these disturbances. Crowds surged on to the street calling for the king to go. He was forced to send Lola into exile and soon abdicated in favour of his son, Maximilian. Lola Montez later married a journalist in San Francisco and had a successful career as a 'Spanish' dancer.

At 10 a.m. on 21 March, Radetzky wrote: 'The streets have been pulled up to an extent you can hardly imagine. Barricades close them by the hundred, even by the thousand . . . The character of the people has been changed as if by magic, and fanaticism has taken hold of every age group, every class, and both sexes . . . The streets to the citadel are closed; and though I repeatedly demolished the barricades, they were always re-erected.'

Around 300 Milanese were killed in the five days' fighting, at least 39 of them women. Despite their bravery, they might never have succeeded in driving the Austrians out on their own. But the peasants in the countryside around Milan had also risen in revolt, and the army of the independent Italian state of Piedmont was advancing towards Milan to attack the Austrians. With all these forces against him, Radetzky reluctantly withdrew from Milan and retreated to the north.

In a single month, revolution had triumphed across the length and breadth of Europe. An old world seemed to be dying in the smoke and blood of the barricades. But could a new world be born from the chaos of revolt?

Lola Montez was born Maria Gilbert in Limerick, Ireland, in 1818. She had a life of adventure, travelling the world. She died in New York at the age of 42.

THE BATTLEGROUNDS OF EUROPE

The spring of 1848 was a time of hope for the working people of Paris. If anything, the revolution had made their sufferings worse. The French economy was disrupted. Poverty and hunger stalked the grim streets and airless courtyards of old Paris. But the workers felt they had bought victory in the February revolution with a sacrifice of blood. Now they expected to benefit from it.

Throughout the poorer districts of the city, political clubs sprang up. Working men went there in the evenings

The French Army and the National Guard parade in front of the Arc de Triomphe, Paris, in spring 1848. This was a period of optimism, when Parisians of all classes joined together to celebrate the revolution.

TIMELINE

1848

27 February
The Provisional Government establishes national workshops for the unemployed.

4 May
The Constituent Assembly, elected by universal suffrage, meets in Paris.

15 May
Demonstrators invade the Assembly, demanding war in aid of Poland.

21 June
The government announces the closing of the national workshops.

23–26 June
'June Days' insurrection in Paris is put down by the army, the National Guard and the *gardes mobiles*.

10 December
Louis Napoleon is elected president of the Second Republic.

to talk and to listen to radical leaders such as Auguste Blanqui and Armand Barbès. In fiery speeches and heated discussions, they speculated on how to end poverty and create a just society. Blanqui advocated a seizure of power, 'the dictatorship of the proletariat'. Others repeated the slogan 'Property is theft'. Many speakers harked back to the glorious days of the 1789 Revolution, when French

A radical speaker holds forth on the future of the revolution in a Parisian political club. Women were allowed in, but only in special seats, separate from the men.

revolutionary armies had conquered Europe and aristocrats' heads had rolled.

About 140,000 Parisians joined these radical political clubs. But most French people did not share the club members' enthusiasm for more revolutionary change. The middle classes, fearing for their property, wanted nothing more to do with revolution. In the French provinces, there was deep suspicion of what was happening far away in Paris.

Conservative peasants, who owned small plots of land, were easily persuaded that Parisian socialists intended to take their land from them.

The members of the Provisional Government that now ruled France were mostly interested in maintaining order. But they did carry out some radical measures. They introduced universal suffrage, giving all adult French males the vote – suddenly there were nine million voters, compared with a quarter of a million under the monarchy. They abolished slavery throughout the French Empire. And they made one major concession to the demands of the Parisian poor – they accepted the 'right to work'.

Immediately after the revolution, Louis Blanc, the only socialist member of the government, was put in charge of setting up national workshops. These offered guaranteed employment to anyone without work. Soon 100,000 unemployed men were enrolled in the workshops, earning two francs a day.

THE NATIONAL WORKSHOPS

Conservative politicians thought of the national workshops as a cheap way of providing relief for the poor and keeping the unemployed off the streets. To social revolutionaries like Louis Blanc, they were a step toward socialist workers' cooperatives. Unemployed workers hoped they would provide real employment.

The workshops became more controversial as time went on. On the whole, they failed to provide proper work. Employers complained that their workers went on strike for higher pay and then signed on at the workshops to support themselves. Conservatives in general thought the workshops encouraged idleness and were centres of political subversion.

EYEWITNESS: A WORKER'S VIEW OF THE WORKSHOPS

On 4 June 1848, an unemployed worker wrote: *'I went into the workshops when I could no longer find bread elsewhere. Since then people have said we were given charity there. But when I went in I did not think that I was becoming a beggar . . . I admit that I have not worked very hard in the national workshops . . . the fact is that, in the national workshops, there was absolutely nothing to do.'*

Above *Parisians place their votes for president in December 1848. The Provisional Government introduced universal male suffrage, giving all adult men the vote.*

Left *Louis Blanc was a socialist who joined the government at the people's request after the February Revolution. Most other members of the government were hostile to socialist ideas such as the national workshops.*

The Assembly against the people

National elections for a Constituent Assembly were held on Easter Sunday. They proved just how conservative the mass of Frenchmen were. Out of 900 deputies elected to the new assembly, only about 80 wanted social reform. Most were solid landowners and professional men, believers in the sacredness of property, the Church and the family. The Provisional Government was replaced by an Executive Commission. No place was found in it for the socialist Louis Blanc.

From the moment the new Assembly met in Paris on 4 May, battle lines were drawn for a showdown. On one side were the newly elected conservatives, men of property and order. On the other was the rebellious population of Paris's poorer districts, people with little to lose but their lives. Everyone assumed a violent struggle would happen soon.

Less then a fortnight after the Assembly's first sitting, round one of the contest was fought. On 15 May an excited crowd broke through a thin cordon of National Guardsmen around the Constituent Assembly and flooded into the building. A few hotheads tried to declare the Assembly dissolved and set up a revolutionary government. The ill-organised demonstrators were soon cleared out. But the event gave the authorities an excuse to act. They arrested most of the fire-eating radical leaders, including Barbès, Blanqui and Albert. Heartened by this success, the conservatives were tempted to seek out another chance to crack down.

The national workshops were the breaking point. To the Parisian poor, these were the only real gain of the revolution, providing at least some money and security for the unemployed. On 21 June, the Executive Commission announced that the workshops were to close. Young unmarried workers were offered the choice of joining the

SOCIALISM IN 1848

The poverty in which workers lived in the early 1800s convinced some Europeans that their society was fundamentally wrong. Why should a few idle rich people have such wealth while the majority lived in misery? Socialists wanted to do something about it.

Many early socialist thinkers were hopelessly Utopian. Charles Fourier (1772–1837) wanted people to live in self-sufficient communities called phalanxes. Everyone would do only work they liked – for example, small boys would collect the garbage because they like playing with dirt. More practical thinkers, like the Comte de Saint-Simon (1760–1825), thought state intervention on behalf of the poor was the

answer. Louis Blanc, the most prominent socialist in 1848, believed workers' cooperatives could replace factories and workshops owned by capitalists.

At street level, socialism in 1848 meant the belief that by taking political power workers could somehow improve their conditions of life radically. One worker, asked why he had taken part in the uprising of June 1848, said, *'I want to ensure that the worker receives the product of his labour, a proportion of which is at present taken away from him by the man who provides the capital. Then there would be no poverty.'* But there were not many socialists in 1848 and they had no effective organisation.

army or being thrown out on the street. Others would be sent out of Paris to work on drainage projects in the unhealthy marshes of Sologne. A deputation of workers was told by a government representative: 'If the workers do not want to leave Paris, we will compel them by force!'

The June Days

On 22 June, the streets of Paris seethed with unrest. Angry crowds milled around the centre of the city. Marching behind national workshop banners, a column of demonstrators chanted, 'Work! Work! Bread! We will not leave!' Alphonse de Lamartine rode through the streets, trying to calm things down by talking to the workers. People spoke to him, he later wrote, 'of their griefs against the Assembly . . . of their misery, of their hunger, of the destitution of their children and of their wives.'

Left *A revolutionary crowd surges into the National Assembly on 15 May 1848, carrying banners marked with the names of their political clubs.*

Below *The romantic poet Alphonse de Lamartine addresses a crowd of Parisians. Lamartine and his liberal colleagues wanted to calm the revolutionary ardour of the Parisian people.*

Above *The French Army blasts rebels' barricades in the Place de la Bastille, Paris, on 25 June 1848.*

Right *These blue-coated French soldiers suffered many casualties during direct frontal assaults on barricades. Many of the rebels had firearms and used them to good effect.*

In the poorer districts of Paris, the barricades went up once more. This time, many of them were massive structures. Author Victor Hugo described one in the Faubourg Saint-Antoine that was 'three storeys high and 700 feet wide', blocking the entrance to three streets at once. The barricades were made of paving stones, barrels, iron bars, wooden beams and whole vehicles – carts and omnibuses perched on the top of the heap. Many of the workers were armed, because since the February revolution they had been allowed to join the National Guard. They had also been expecting a fight. On 23 June about 20,000 rebels settled down behind the barricades to await the inevitable attack. Their slogan was 'Liberty or death'.

THE COMMUNIST MANIFESTO

It was during the 1848 revolution that an obscure German socialist, Karl Marx, and his colleague Friedrich Engels published the *Communist Manifesto*. It appealed to the new industrial working class to rise up and overthrow existing society: *'The workers have nothing to lose . . . but their chains. They have a world to gain. Workers of the world, unite!'*

Marx and Engels had little influence on the 1848 revolution. But Marx was right to say that 'the spectre of Communism' haunted Europe. Marx's communism was against religion, the family and private property. Communism represented everything the middle classes feared most.

Karl Marx believed the 1848 revolutions showed his theory of class war was right: workers had to fight capitalists for political power.

In February, an enfeebled monarchy had collapsed at the sight of the barricades. But the government of June had been elected by the French people. It had the will, as well as the force, to crush the insurrection. Even many sincere Republicans who genuinely sympathised with the sufferings of the poor believed they had to support the democratically elected Assembly against the rebels.

The National Guardsmen from the middle-class districts of Paris were spoiling for a fight. The newly built railways brought 100,000 Guardsmen up from the provinces, eager to sort out the Parisian revolutionaries. The peasant recruits of the regular army could be relied on to obey their orders. Even among the working people of Paris, the rebels had only limited support. Since February, over 15,000 of the young unemployed – often youths 14 or 15 years old – had been enrolled as paramilitary *gardes mobiles*. They were to prove the fiercest fighters against their working-class brothers on the other side of the barricades.

On 24 June the Assembly declared a state of siege in Paris. General Louis Cavaignac, the Minister of Defence, was made virtual military dictator. Cavaignac hated the revolutionaries passionately. He set out to crush the uprising with overwhelming force. He concentrated his troops – regular army, National Guard and *gardes mobiles* – in a series of frontal assaults on the barricades.

For three days Paris was torn by savage fighting. When government troops attacked, the rebels fired volleys over the top of the barricades and from upstairs windows in flanking buildings. Rushing across open squares or from doorway to doorway up narrow streets, the soldiers took what cover they could. Many fell to the rebel fire.

But the army had artillery. If they could manoeuver their cannon into position to fire on the barricades, the effect would be devastating. A woman described how buildings were demolished: 'One of them had no part standing but the wall on which the looking glass remained unbroken.' It was impossible to imagine, she wrote, 'how anyone escaped the butchery committed there.'

Above *General Cavaignac appeals to the National Assembly for support against the revolutionaries. He was given almost total power to crush the June uprising by force and later became known as 'the Butcher of Paris'.*

EYEWITNESS: THE REBELS IN THE JUNE DAYS

Frightened 'respectable' French citizens saw the rebellious poor as, in the words of one journalist, *'barbarians, desperados emerging from their lairs for massacre and looting, and odious partisans of those wild doctrines that the family is only a word and property naught but theft.'*

The socialist Louis Blanc saw them differently: *'The worker did not take up arms because of his own sufferings. He did so because he felt for his old father, his wife, his children and his workmates. He protested against the prolongation of poverty, not just because it is torture to the body, but because it is oppression to the soul.'*

Right *Revolutionaries lie dying in the streets of Paris. This painting is by the artist Ernest Meissonier, who took part in the fighting.*

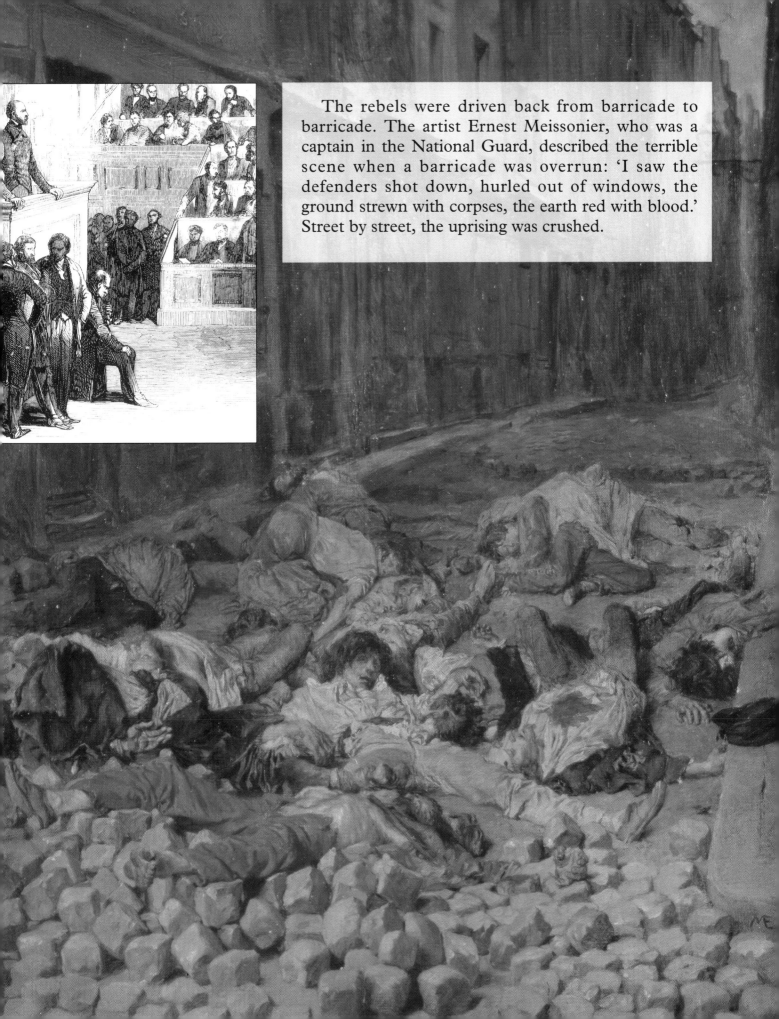

The rebels were driven back from barricade to barricade. The artist Ernest Meissonier, who was a captain in the National Guard, described the terrible scene when a barricade was overrun: 'I saw the defenders shot down, hurled out of windows, the ground strewn with corpses, the earth red with blood.' Street by street, the uprising was crushed.

About 500 rebels died on the barricades. But that was the lesser part of the killing. Around 3,000 more were massacred in cold blood, mercilessly hunted down through the alleyways of Paris. Firing squads shot down prisoners outside the Hotel de Ville, Paris's town hall. Other killings were more casual. When a man was captured without a gun, the soldiers would sniff his ear for gunpowder. If they smelt the powder, proving the man had fired a gun, he was put up against a wall and shot.

Parisians suspected of putting up posters supporting revolution are searched by General Cavaignac's men. Around 3,000 rebels were massacred in cold blood during the June Days insurrection, and 12,000 more were imprisoned.

The aftermath of repression

About 12,000 rebels were arrested and imprisoned, often packed into stinking overcrowded cells where the dead and dying were left to lie among the living. Many were shot by trigger-happy guards while 'trying to escape'. Of those who came to trial, thousands were deported to labour camps in Algeria – which was, for many, a sentence of death.

In this carnage conservatives saw the triumph of civilisation over barbarism, of order over anarchy. To the people of the poor quarters of Paris, it was a catastrophe. They had to try to rebuild their lives – many widowed or orphaned – amid the bullet-scarred, shell-raked streets.

The following December there were elections for a president to head the Second Republic. Alexandre Ledru-Rollin, the leading radical, polled 370,000 votes. A million people voted for Cavaignac, the 'Butcher of Paris'. But the overwhelming winner was Louis Napoleon, nephew of the great French emperor, with over five million votes. To most people, Louis Napoleon represented order and strong government. By voting for him, the French people buried the revolution.

LOUIS NAPOLEON

Louis Napoleon was born in 1808, the nephew of the great Napoleon Bonaparte. In 1840 he was imprisoned after a failed attempt to seize power in France by force. He escaped six years later and fled to England. In 1848, trading on his name, he convinced millions of Frenchmen that he was the president who could restore order and give France back its glory. Even workers voted for him, believing he was on the side of 'the people'.

His contemporary Alexis de Tocqueville called Louis Napoleon 'an enigmatic, sombre, insignificant numskull.' But Louis made himself emperor of France in 1852 and ruled the country as Napoleon III until 1870, when defeat by Prussia brought down his régime.

Louis Napoleon was often called 'the Little Napoleon' to distinguish him from his uncle, 'the Great Napoleon' Bonaparte. The French voted him into power hoping he would save them from anarchy.

THE DEFEAT OF THE REVOLUTIONS

The disasters that befell the revolutionaries in France were a foretaste of what was to happen in the rest of Europe. In the heady days of February and March 1848, the kings, emperors and aristocrats had been on the run. But they soon recovered their nerve and fought back. And the revolutionaries often proved their own worst enemies.

The Frankfurt talking shop

In Germany, a national parliament met at Frankfurt in May 1848. It was an assembly of civil servants, lawyers, professors and schoolteachers. They agreed on the middle-class demands for equality before the law, a career open to talents and a free press. But they could agree on little else. Some wanted Germany to be a democratic republic. Others wanted a federation of the existing German princedoms. Some wanted Germany to be led by Prussia. Others wanted Austria included in the new federation.

As their debates dragged on interminably in the Frankfurt 'talking shop', it became obvious that these German liberals had no power at all. They had no army, and they could not appeal for popular support because they were afraid that the workers would take power for themselves. Whenever there were strikes, riots or disturbances, the liberals immediately wanted soldiers brought in to maintain order. And these soldiers belonged to liberalism's enemies, the king of Prussia and the Austrian emperor.

Above Deputies file into Paulskirche, Frankfurt, for the opening of the German national parliament in May 1848.

Right The German national parliament met in fine surroundings, but it had no power. A year of talk produced no positive results.

TIMELINE

1848

18 May
The German assembly meets at Frankfurt.

16 June
Windischgrätz bombards Prague, where the Pan-Slav Congress is gathered.

23 July
The Austrians defeat the Italians at the Battle of Custozza.

6 October
The beginning of the October Days uprising in Vienna.

1 November
Windischgrätz retakes Vienna for the Habsburgs.

24 November
The Pope flees from Rome.

1849

9 February
Mazzini establishes the Roman Republic.

23 March
The Austrians defeat the Italians at the Battle of Novarra.

3 April
The king of Prussia rejects the offer of the German throne from the Frankfurt assembly.

14 April
Kossuth declares Hungary an independent republic.

3 July
French forces occupy Rome, ending the Roman Republic.

13 August
The Hungarians surrender to the Russian Army.

22 August
Venice surrenders to the Austrians.

King Frederick William IV of Prussia despised the Frankfurt assembly. When they offered him the throne of a united Germany, he refused it.

The Prussian king, Frederick William IV, had soon pulled himself together after his surrender to the revolution in March. Backed by the *junkers* – the haughty landowners of Prussia – he set about reversing the liberal reforms he had been forced to grant. By December 1848 he felt strong enough to abolish the elected assembly in Berlin and resume virtually absolute rule.

In March 1849 the Frankfurt assembly finally reached agreement, after almost a year of debate. Ironically, what they agreed was to invite the anti-liberal Prussian king to become ruler of a new federal Germany. The king scuppered all their plans by simply refusing. He would not accept a crown from the hands of an elected assembly. With that, the liberals' attempt to make a united Germany collapsed. The Frankfurt assembly fell apart.

Saving the Habsburg Empire

The Habsburg rulers of Austria had a much tougher battle to fight. After the first uprising in March, armed workers and students held the upper hand in the Austrian capital, Vienna. They forced the emperor to authorise the election of a Constituent Assembly. Meanwhile, the Austrian emperor's Slav and Hungarian subjects were demanding self-rule.

If the enemies of the emperor had been united, they might have triumphed. But they were fatally divided. The imperial forces were able to pick them off one by one, or even set them against one another. The first imperial success came in June. A congress of Slavs had gathered in Prague to demand a measure of self-rule for the different Slav peoples. Prince Alfred von Windischgrätz, the imperial governor of Moravia, found an excuse to bombard the city with artillery. After that, little more was heard of Slav self-rule.

Above *Prince Alfred von Windischgrätz suppressed the Slav congress in Prague with an artillery bombardment.*

The Hungarians were made of sterner stuff. Inspired by their fiery leader, Lajos Kossuth, they built on their early successes. A Hungarian parliament was elected in July and soon voted to raise its own army. But the Hungarians leading this drive for self-rule were aristocrats and landowners. They were hated by other peoples – chiefly Croats and Romanians – living in the part of the Austrian Empire they now proposed to rule. The Austrians craftily set nation against nation. Baron Josip Jellacic, a Croat nobleman, was encouraged to raise Croatia in revolt against the Hungarians. In September, Jellacic led an army towards the Hungarian capital, Budapest.

Now the Austrian Empire's struggle for survival reached its climax. The Austrians decided to send in their own army to subdue the Hungarians. Kossuth was made virtual dictator of Hungary and vigorously organised its defence. On 6 October students and workers in the Austrian capital staged a revolt in support of the Hungarians. They tried to stop troops being sent from Vienna. The Austrian Minister of War, Count Latour, was lynched. The propertied classes panicked. About 100,000 of them fled from Vienna. So did the emperor's family and the Constituent Assembly.

Left *Armed railway workers, led by uniformed students of the Academic Legion, march towards the centre of Vienna. Together, workers and students seized control of the city.*

Right *Count Latour, the Austrian Minister of War, was hanged from a lamppost by an angry crowd on 6 October 1848. As a result, many middle-class people who had once backed the revolution feared for their lives and fled Vienna.*

LAJOS KOSSUTH

Kossuth was a Hungarian aristocrat. Before 1848 he already had a reputation as a passionate nationalist. His political activities had landed him in an Austrian prison. In September 1848 he became virtual dictator of Hungary, leading his people in their desperate struggle for self-rule. When the Hungarians surrendered in August 1849, Kossuth fled to Turkey. He spent the rest of his life in exile in Britain, Italy and the United States.

Above *Lajos Kossuth, a Hungarian national hero, inspired his nation's resistance to Austria. This portrait shows him as an old man, living in exile.*

Left *This spectacular barricade in the middle of Vienna had a whole wooden cart built into it. Women played a leading part in building the barricades and staffing them.*

The students and workers did what they could to prepare a defence of Vienna against the inevitable counterattack by the Austrian Army. But they knew their only real hope lay in a victory for the Hungarians. On 23 October, Windischgrätz began an assault on Vienna. As he blasted his way into the city, Kossuth's troops advanced to within a few miles of the suburbs. But they never linked up with the revolutionaries inside Vienna. By 1 November the city was firmly in the hands of the Austrian authorities. About 5,000 rebels had died on the bloodstained streets.

Imperial power was restored in Austria. In December the feeble-minded Emperor Ferdinand was persuaded to abdicate, and his young nephew Franz Josef took the throne. He was destined to remain emperor for almost 70 years.

Hungary fights on

The war against the isolated Hungarians continued relentlessly. In January 1849 Budapest fell to Windischgrätz's army, but the Hungarian government retreated to the town of Debrecem and fought on. The Hungarian army was brilliantly led by Arthur von Gorgey. Through March and April 1849 it repeatedly defeated the Austrians. The Austrian Army was harassed by Hungarian peasants who fought their own guerrilla war, inspired by Kossuth's rousing leadership. On 14 April Kossuth declared Hungary an independent republic.

As a last resort, the Austrian emperor appealed to the tsar of Russia for assistance. The tsar, who hated all revolutionaries, was only too glad to help. Soon, a 100,000-strong Russian army was marching across the plains of Hungary. The Hungarians were overwhelmed by force of numbers. On 13 August 1849, facing inevitable defeat, Gorgey surrendered to the Russians. Kossuth escaped, but the Austrians wreaked a terrible vengeance on other leaders of the revolt. Thirteen Hungarian generals were shot, and thousands of Hungarians were sent to rot in Austria's notorious prisons.

Right *Giuseppe Mazzini's ideas were considered so dangerous that people were shot simply for reading what he wrote.*

Below *Hungarian peasants in traditional dress support the rebel Hungarian Army.*

The fate of Italy

In the spring of 1848 Italy seemed to have every chance of freeing itself from foreign rule. The Austrian army was on the run, chased out of Venice and Milan. The leading advocate of Italian nationalism, Giuseppe Mazzini, returned from exile in France. He felt that the moment for a united Italy had come.

But Italy's rulers did not share Mazzini's enthusiasm. Pope Pius IX and King Ferdinand II at first succumbed to popular pressure to send armies to fight against the Austrians. They soon backed down, however. Ferdinand brought his troops home, using them instead to suppress the revolution in Naples and Sicily. The Pope also denounced the war against Austria, blandly announcing, 'We seek after and embrace all races, peoples and nations, with equal devotion of paternal love.'

The revolution in Italy was defeated during 1848 and 1849. The Austrians attacked in the north, retaking Milan and Venice; the French sent an army to crush the Roman Republic; and King Ferdinand won back control of Naples and Sicily.

King Charles Albert of Piedmont was ready to fight Austria, but not from any love of liberty. His ambition was to extend his domains. He insisted that when the war was won, Milan and Venice should come under his rule. In fact, he was quite incapable of defeating the Austrian General Radetzky. Charles Albert was hesitant and his army was inefficient. Radetzky had time to regroup his forces and trounced the Italians at the Battle of Custozza on 23 July.

The Italian revolution began to fall apart. After the defeat at Custozza, Mazzini tried to organise popular resistance in Milan. But, abandoned by Charles Albert, the city that had fought so gloriously in March allowed their foreign rulers to return without a fight. The Austrian army used the whip and the firing squad to wreak vengeance on those Milanese who had revolted against their rule.

Charles Albert wavered between negotiating peace with Austria and continuing the fight. Finally, on 23 March 1849, the Italian army suffered a further crushing defeat at Navarra. The humiliated Charles Albert abdicated and his son Victor Emmanuel took the throne. In northern Italy, only Venice still held out under Austrian blockade.

Above Radicals opposed to Bourbon King Ferdinand II shoot down at the army in the streets of Naples.

The Roman Republic

After failing to lead a nationalist revolution in Milan, Mazzini moved on to Rome. Unemployment, poverty and hunger were still fuelling a blaze of popular discontent across the centre of Italy. In Rome discontent was doubled by anger against the Pope, who was seen as having betrayed the cause of liberty and Italian nationalism.

On 15 November 1848 the Pope's leading minister, Count Pellegrino Rossi, was assassinated – stabbed in the neck while surrounded by an angry Roman crowd. The following day the Pope's palace was attacked. In fear of his life, the Pope fled the city, taking refuge at Gaeta in the kingdom of Naples.

A radical government took power in Rome and called democratic elections. The Pope denounced the elections as 'abominable, monstrous, illegal, impious, absurd, sacrilegious and outrageous.' They were an overwhelming victory for the radicals. The Inquisition and censorship were abolished, Church land was nationalised and the unemployed were given work on public projects. In February 1849, the former Papal States became the Roman Republic.

Aid for the Pope came from a rather unexpected quarter. Louis Napoleon, now president of France, wanted to increase his popularity among French Catholics and win some cheap military glory. He sent an invasion force under General Oudinot to restore Rome to the Pope.

To organise the defence of the city in this grave emergency, the Roman Republic turned to Mazzini. He led a triumvirate – a three-man ruling council. The forces at his disposal did not look promising. There were only a few thousand soldiers of the former papal army and a citizens' National Guard of dubious worth.

Romans prepare to resist the advancing French troops. Uniformed soldiers, Garibaldi's guerrillas and ordinary citizens fought side by side.

GIUSEPPE GARIBALDI

Giuseppe Garibaldi was born in 1807 in Nice, then an Italian port. Garibaldi was an uneducated sailor. He took part in a failed nationalist uprising in 1834. Under risk of arrest, he fled to exile in South America. There he learned the art of guerrilla fighting in wars on the pampas. The exploits of the Italian Legion he formed in Uruguay brought him his first fame.

In 1848 he returned to Italy and led the Republican forces in Rome. After defeat he fled to exile once more, this time in the United States. But in 1860 he boldly landed in Sicily with 1,000 men – the 'Red Shirts' – and conquered southern Italy, trouncing the Bourbon Army. Everywhere he inspired popular enthusiasm. An eyewitness wrote, *'When the populace sees him they take fire. There is a magic in his look and in his name.'*

He was denied the full fruits of victory, however. A lifelong enemy of kings, he had to hand over the lands he had conquered to the new king of Italy. And he never achieved his ambition of conquering Rome. He tried twice more, in 1862 and 1867, but was defeated both times.

Garibaldi was one of the most romantic figures of the nineteenth century. He was never corrupted by money or power and was an admirer of freedom-loving people everywhere.

Fortunately, three days before the French began their attack, Giuseppe Garibaldi arrived in the city at the head of his dedicated band of irregulars. With daggers in their belts, ill-kempt beards and fierce, dusty faces, the *Garibaldini* looked like a gang of bandits. But the charismatic presence of their bearded, long-haired leader inspired a rush of students and artists to volunteer to bear arms. Another legion of fighters arrived from Milan, led by Angelo Masina, an aristocrat who was not prepared to accept the reimposition of Austrian rule.

EYEWITNESS: GARIBALDI'S FAREWELL

Before leaving Rome at the end of June 1849, Garibaldi addressed the crowd in St Peter's Square. Muddy and bloodstained from the battle, he appealed for volunteers to continue the war for Italian freedom: *'I ask nothing of them but a heart filled with love for our country. They will have no pay, no provisions and no rest. I offer hunger, cold, forced marches, battles and death. Whoever is not satisfied with such a life must remain behind. He who has the name of Italy not only on his lips but in his heart, let him follow me.'*

On 30 April 1849, the battle for Rome began. Inexperienced student volunteers, *Garibaldini* guerrillas and former papal troops fought side by side to resist the first French assault. There was heavy slaughter in the pleasant public gardens at the edge of Rome as the fighting swayed back and forth. Bayonetted Frenchmen lay in heaps under the flowering rose bushes. Garibaldi was seen in the thick of the fighting on his distinctive white horse – he received a bullet wound in the side. But the French were driven back.

General Oudinot decided he would need much stronger forces to conquer these fierce defenders. He did not resume the offensive until the beginning of June, by which time he had 30,000 heavily armed troops at his disposal. On 3 June, in the most bitter fighting of the conflict, the French occupied and held key positions overlooking Rome. This enabled them to put the city under continual artillery bombardment. The defenders valiantly held the line of the city walls, but with each day their

Below *Despite valiant defence by the Romans, French troops sent by Louis Napoleon eventually marched into Rome and restored power to the Pope.*

position weakened. On the moonless night of 30 June, the French broke through the walls and into the city.

The Roman parliament hastily assembled and voted to surrender. Mazzini, who had wanted a fight to the death, resigned. Garibaldi led a small force out of the city to continue the fight elsewhere – a futile but heroic gesture. The French took over Rome, facing the insults of a sullen, beaten people. Soon the Pope was restored to his earthly throne.

The Venetian Republic

The last toehold of the revolution in Italy was in Venice. Under the leadership of Daniel Manin, the Venetians resisted three months of bombardment by Austrian artillery and a blockade that brought them near to starvation. But on 22 August 1849 they, too, surrendered. The revolutions that had begun in 1848 were over.

Above *Daniel Manin – pictured proclaiming the Venetian Republic in St Mark's Square, Venice, on 23 March 1848 – led the Republic of Venice until its surrender in August 1849.*

WHY DID THE REVOLUTIONS FAIL?

There were four main reasons why the 1848 revolutions ended in failure. First, the revolutionaries were divided. The middle-class liberals had different aims from the working-class radicals. The different nationalities in the Habsburg Empire also disagreed violently – Slavs and Romanians fought Hungarians, Germans despised Slavs.

Second, the peasants who made up the majority of the population of Europe were hardly involved in the revolutions at all. In many places they were indifferent or counter-revolutionary.

Third, once they recovered from the shock of the first uprisings, the old authorities realised they had all the essentials of power intact. In particular, they had armed forces that were ready to obey orders and put down rebellion.

Finally, the middle classes always preferred the security of order to the uncertainty of revolution in the end. Disorder was bad for business. Ultimately, most property owners would back any firm ruler against a workers' uprising that threatened their property.

AFTERMATH AND CONSEQUENCES

On 2 December 1851, President Louis Napoleon carried out a military *coup d'état* in Paris. His *coup* ended the Second Republic and founded the Second Empire, with himself as emperor. The democratically elected National Assembly was dissolved. The few protestors who threw up barricades or demonstrated in the streets were shot down mercilessly.

The revolutions of 1848 had failed utterly. By 1851 monarchs and emperors were in control throughout Europe. There had been a few positive achievements. Feudal dues and forced labour for peasants had been abolished in the Austrian lands. In France, the new Emperor Napoleon III kept universal male suffrage – although elections were strictly controlled to make sure the right person won.

But the idealistic revolutionary aspirations to change

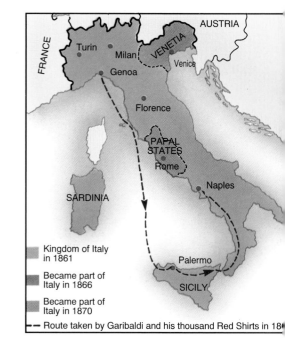

Kingdom of Italy in 1861

Became part of Italy in 1866

Became part of Italy in 1870

- - - Route taken by Garibaldi and his thousand Red Shirts in 18

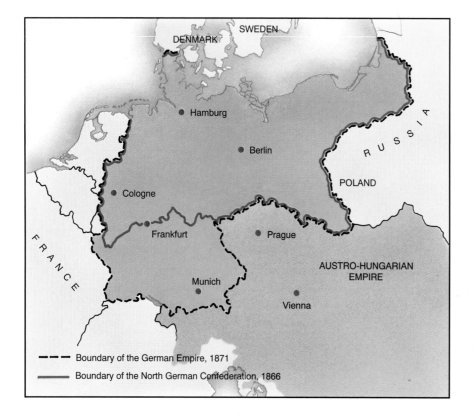

Boundary of the German Empire, 1871

Boundary of the North German Confederation, 1866

Above *Most of Italy was unified in 1861 under the King of Piedmont and Sardinia, Victor Emmanuelle II. Venice joined the Italian kingdom in 1866 and unification was completed in 1870 with the conquest of Rome.*

Left *Germany was eventually unified by the power of the Prussian Army. In 1866 the Prussians defeated Austria and formed a North German Confederation. In 1871, after defeating France, Prussia founded the German Empire.*

the world had come to nothing. The leading revolutionaries were in prison, in exile or dead. Many disappointed working people who had invested their hopes in the revolution joined the flood of emigrants crossing the Atlantic to make new lives for themselves in the freer atmosphere of the New World

Apart from one major outbreak – the Paris Commune of 1870 to 1871 – there were no more serious revolutionary upheavals in Europe for 70 years. One reason was economic. The 1840s were the last decade in European history when people went hungry in peacetime. From the 1850s, industry and technology grew spectacularly. The optimistic new world of apparently limitless progress was celebrated by the Great Exhibition held in London in 1851.

Although people shared in this material progress unequally, all benefited to some degree. Cities like London and Paris were transformed by proper sewerage and street lighting. There were no more cholera epidemics. Many old working-class slums, especially in Paris, were cleared away and replaced by broad boulevards – much less suitable for barricades and street fighting.

A Hungarian patriot is prepared for execution by firing squad after the defeat of the revolution. In other countries, too, defeated rebels were shot, imprisoned or driven into exile.

Many of the changes for which the revolutionaries of 1848 had fought came about in one form or another. By the 1870s, every major European country except Russia had an elected parliament and more or less respected basic human freedoms. Radical demands of 1848, such as universal education, became standard features of European states.

Revolutionary dreamers and activists still existed after 1848, as did the gross inequality and social injustice that they wanted to end. But the main thrust of socialism and radicalism went into mass movements that worked for peaceful, gradual change. By the twentieth century, trade unions and socialist political parties had become a normal part of the European scene. Even Marxists thought they would win power by the vote, not on the barricades. A few individuals still advocated a revolutionary seizure of power by the workers, but they seemed an old-fashioned irrelevance – until one of them, Vladimir Ilyich Lenin, actually succeeded in doing so in 1917.

Above A crowd gathers in St Marks Square, Venice, in 1867 to see Garibaldi. He again attempted to conquer Rome in that year, but was defeated.

Right The Russian revolutionaries of 1917 show off their weapons. They were determined not to lose their fight, as the revolutionaries of 1848 had done.

NATIONALISM AFTER 1848

Most of the nationalist aspirations of 1848 were fulfilled within the following quarter century – but not by revolution. Italian unity was achieved under the Piedmontese king, Victor Emmanuel II, and his prime minister, Camillo Cavour. With the help of the French Army, the Piedmontese defeated the Austrians in 1859. Garibaldi invaded Sicily the following year and defeated King Ferdinand. Victor Emmanuel became the king of Italy in 1861, adding Venice to his kingdom in 1866 and, finally, Rome in 1870.

Germany was united largely through the 'blood and iron' policy of the Prussian chancellor, Otto von Bismarck. By winning wars against Austria in 1866 and France in 1870 to 1871, he created the German Empire, with the Prussian king as its ruler. The new Germany was the most powerful country in Europe, an authoritarian and militarised state.

The multinational Habsburg Empire, shorn of its Italian provinces, continued to rule in Vienna until 1918. It survived by making concessions to different national groups and keeping them divided. Hungary was given semi-independence in 1867, when the empire was renamed Austro-Hungary. This was as much as most of the Hungarian rebels of 1848 had ever wanted.

GLOSSARY

Absolute rule Many kings and emperors had unlimited power. They could change any law or overrule it. There was no parliament or constitution to put a check on their authority. They were absolute rulers.

Aristocrat Aristocrats were the traditional ruling group in European countries. They were mostly owners of large areas of land. They had titles like 'duke' or 'lord' which they had inherited from their parents. In the 1800s the aristocrats were slowly losing power to the middle classes, who made money out of industry and trade instead of land.

Artisan Artisans were skilled workmen who made goods such as shoes or furniture. Artisans worked in small workshops and made things by hand, using their own tools. During the 1800s, most artisans were driven out of business by large factories, which mass-produced the same goods more cheaply by machine, using unskilled workers.

Cholera Cholera is a killer disease spread by lack of sanitation. It ravaged the population of the filthy cities of Europe in the early 1800s.

Communism Communism is an extreme form of socialism. Communists believe that eventually all private property will be abolished. People will work harmoniously together instead of competing with or exploiting each other. Everyone will have what they need in life. In the twentieth century, governments professing communism became brutal dictatorships.

Constitution A constitution is a set of rules saying how a society is to be governed. A constitution limits the power of a government and gives citizens rights that they can uphold in court.

Cooperatives Cooperatives are workplaces in which everything is owned in common by the workers. There is no employer and any profits are shared among the workforce.

Democracy Democracy is a system of government in which the rulers are elected by the people whom they rule.

Empire An empire is usually a collection of different peoples or lands ruled by a single ruler or government. In some cases, however, countries call themselves 'empires' because it sounds more grand.

Liberals In the 1800s, liberals were people who wanted basic individual freedoms, such as the right to say and write what they thought, and the right to a fair trial. They thought every country should have a parliament and a constitution. But most liberals were opposed to socialism and democracy. They thought the right to vote should be restricted to the middle classes.

Nationalism Nationalism is the belief that people with the same language and traditions should live together in a single state with its own national government.

Peasant A peasant is a rural worker who owns only a small amount of land or no land at all. In 1848, the majority of the population in all countries on the European mainland were peasants.

Radical Radical is a general term for people who want a fundamental change in politics or society, rather than minor reforms.

Republic A republic is a country governed by a president or a prime minister, instead of a king or emperor. Republics were very unusual in Europe in the 1800s. Almost all countries were headed by monarchs.

Self-rule Self-rule is a term used for a measure of independence given to a country within an empire. The country is allowed to run its own internal affairs, but still accepts the foreign ruler as its head of state.

Socialist In the 1800s, different socialists believed different things. But in general socialists were against competition and in favour of cooperation. They believed workers were exploited by their employers and wanted to defend their rights and interests. Socialists wanted more equality of wealth and thought the state should take over at least the major industries and banks. They thought the state could run the economy for the benefit of everybody.

Universal suffrage Universal suffrage means everyone having the right to vote in elections. In practice, however, there are always limits to voting. In the 1800s, when people said 'universal suffrage' they meant votes for all men over the age of 21. Women did not get the right to vote in Europe until the twentieth century.

FURTHER INFORMATION

BOOKS

Novels

Charles Dickens, *Oliver Twist*, Puffin (1994)
This novel and other Dickens classics are worth reading for a background feel of the period. They show the poverty and squalor of life in nineteenth-century cities, and the harsh attitude that many of the better-off people adopted toward the poor.

Gustave Flaubert, *Sentimental Education*, Penguin (1964)
Flaubert was the greatest French novelist of this period. *Sentimental Education* is the story of the life and loves of a young man making his way in Paris in the 1840s. The second half of the book centres around the 1848 revolution, including a harrowing description of the repression of the June Days uprising.

Christopher Hibbert, *Garibaldi and His Enemies*, Penguin (1987)
This is a good popular account of Garibaldi's exploits.

Victor Hugo, *Les Misérables*, Penguin (1982)
Victor Hugo's enormous novel paints the most vivid picture of life among the poor in Paris during this period. It includes an exciting description of the fighting on the barricades in 1848.

Giuseppe Lampedusa, *The Leopard*, Everyman (1991)
This sophisticated Italian novel tells the story of an aristocratic family in Sicily before and after Garibaldi's invasion in 1860. It gives a good idea of the lifestyles and political tensions of the times.

Leonardo Sciascia, 'Forty-Eight', in *The Wine-Dark Sea*
The story of a Sicilian nobleman who is constantly trying to keep in with whoever is in power. Out of print but available from libraries.

Non-fiction

Michael Pollard, *The 19th Century*, Volume 7 of the *Illustrated History of the World*, Simon and Schuster (1992)
This general history book for young readers offers solid background information on the period. It has some good details and illustrations of the 1848 revolutions and their leading personalities.

A. J. P. Taylor, *Revolutions and Revolutionaries*, Hamish Hamilton (1980)
Taylor is a quirky historian whose books are always readable. This volume includes an excellent brief account of the 1848 revolutions and the leading revolutionaries involved. It has exciting pictures of the main events. The book is probably more likely to be available from libraries than bookshops.

FILMS AND PLAYS

The Leopard (1963)
The film version of Lampedusa's novel stars Burt Lancaster and Claudia Cardinale. Available on video.

Les Misérables
Seeing the musical stage version of Hugo's epic is the most painless way of taking a run through French history at this period. It captures the optimism and the tragedy of 1848.

Oliver Twist (1948)
David Lean's black-and-white version of *Oliver Twist* is still gripping today. Catch it on afternoon television, or perhaps on video.

INDEX